Prove

Brown Girl Proverb: This Goes Out To All The Women And The Secrets They Keep

Thank you for supporting!

Riya!

Lermesha Stubblefield

Preface

I've wanted to write a book since I was about ten years old. I always knew that I wanted to tell a story about my life. I also knew that I wanted to share my story so that it would eventually help someone. However, at ten years old you don't have too much shit to tell or too much advice to give. So here I am, eleven years later with a hell of a lot to say. This book is only seven chapters for a reason. Seven is the number of completion. When I was done writing this book I wanted to feel as though it was complete. I wanted to be sure I set out to do what I was supposed to do. Also, I have terrible anxiety and would have stressed myself out trying to figure out when to stop writing! So, this worked out great. I expected this process to be, at least, a year long. But, it took me only seven months to write, rewrite, and edit this entire body of work. There's that number seven, again. And believe me when I say that was unintentional as hell, but God works in mysterious ways. Nothing I have written was out of anger or disrespect, but mostly out of pain and growth. I've read a million books while growing up, and each of them have taught me and helped me through different things. I wanted to be a blessing to readers out there just as the authors of those books were blessings to me. My favorite would most definitely be Sister Souljah. The Coldest Winter Ever was the first book of hers that I'd read. I was fourteen. That book was the realest thing that I'd laid my eyes on and I was hooked on her ever since. The most recent book of hers that I've read was No Disrespect. This is by far the best book I've ever read. I've never related to someone in so many ways before. After I was done reading, I wanted to call her up and thank her! At that moment, I knew I wanted to have the same impact on some young man or young woman that she had, had on me. This is how Brown Girl Proverb was born.

The title fits perfectly with what I was trying to accomplish. It is also very specific to me, being as though I am a brown girl and the book of Proverbs is home to some of my favorite scriptures. One of which I have tattooed: Proverb 31:25 She is clothed with strength and dignity and she laughs without fear of the future. It is also the last chapter of the Old Testament—completion. When I decided to get that scripture tattooed on me, I was coming out of a very heavy state of depression. I was very lost. I came across this scripture, and I became emotionally attached to it. In this same moment, I started recognizing small things that I realized were starting to make me happy. For instance, the color yellow and sunflowers (hence the cover of this book). Yellow symbolizes happiness, positivity, clarity, and enlightenment. These were all things I have sought out in my life. According to the seven chakras, the sunflower symbolizes longevity and willingness to stick things out during periods of difficulty. This is why I am a strong believer in purpose. All of these things were aligning at different moments for different reasons, yet they all were connected somehow. Not by luck, but by God.

So, I hope that after reading this book things start to align with your life as well.

Favor, Peace & Blessings,
Mimi

Acknowledgments

Here's to a new thing. Thank you to Novi Brown. Thank you to Hill Harper. Thank you to poetry. Thank you to literature. Thank you to Love. Thank you to pain. Thank you to Sister Souljah. Thank you to Pastor Sarah Jakes Roberts. Thank you to failure. Thank you to Pastor Hannah. Thank you to success. Thank you to Me. Thank you to God.
Here's to my *greatness*.

In Loving Memory of Jamela "Baby J" Anthony
Your proverb is one that'll be told forever.

Prologue

Just a heads up, none of what I mention throughout these next fifty plus pages will be considered "cute", "sparkly", "girly", sugar coated or made easy to swallow. If I were to have taken that route, I wouldn't be giving you all the *real* shit. So this is a heads up to whomever may be shocked and, in turn, become uncomfortable with what they are about to read or what they've read so far: I am grown. I curse a lot. I am vulgar. I am honest. I believe in GOD. I speak with love. My words are poetic. I am a healer. I do not mislead, yet, often misinterpreted. I am ghetto as hell. I am smart as hell. I am funny as hell. I am eccentric. I am classy. I choose metaphorical descriptions over literal ones. I am sensitive, I feel everything. You don't like it? You don't have to, but at least hear me out. These are lessons intended to bring you comfort, alignment and enlightenment. I've learned that a sense of familiarity tends to guide a lost mind, a lost heart and a lost spirit. I hope that after reading about my journey you'll either reflect on or move easier through yours. Take what you need, agree with what you feel, take note of what you never knew and most importantly, pass this on. Are you ready? Let us begin.

Table Of Contents

1. SOME REAL SH*T

BE CONSISTENT IN SPITE OF COMPLICATIONS

Why should you trust me, of all the brown girls in the world, to give you the guidance you never realized you needed? There are approximately seventeen thousand active black psychologists in the United States; for every active male black psychologist there are 5.8 active female black psychologists. I don't fall into any of those categories, but I've learned at a very young age that I don't have to be academically qualified to be considered smart or intelligent. I do not need a degree to tell you some *real* shit. I do not need a license to give you advice on how to heal yourself, all I need is experience. Experience is time's most reliable subject. Since I've gone through my obstacles, I can tell you how to spot yours before they come, how to handle them when they get to you and how to move past them once they've overstayed their welcome.

Now, you're probably thinking, "You must think you're Iyanla Vanzant or some shit like that?" but that's not it at all. I'm not setting out to fix your life, instead I am here to make sure you are *aware* of what needs to be tended to. I'm here to help you figure some shit out, you know? I'm that little muthafucka on your shoulder telling you to watch out while also nursing you back to health if you get hit with an issue. In my twenty-one years I've dealt with a lot of pain, learned plenty of lessons, lost a lot of people, gained a handful of friends, received a plethora of blessings and so forth—and *this* is why you should trust me. However, do not confuse "to trust me" with "agreeing with me", because I'm not asking you to do so. But even if you do not agree, I pray that you are willing to gain new perspectives. Look at things from my point of view. Read with the intentions to understand, rather than to respond. If you've been keeping track already, I just brought up two very important things that should be noted: Experience and Perspective. Jot that down.

Like I said earlier, I'm only twenty-one. But, Aaliyah said it best, "Age ain't nuthin' but a numba." But, it wasn't until year twenty-one that a lot of things were brought to my attention. I experienced all the good, the bad, the ugly, the beautiful, the most difficult— a lot of shit. I saw God twist and turn me, flip me upside down, reshape me, break my foundation and start me from scratch. Throughout that process, separation was the most medicinal step I could've taken. Discernment and acceptance have kept me at my most content state. I'm legitimately okay! I have a small village, but a prayerful village. It's nothing anyone can say or do at this point to shift my growth or my spirit. I'm what's best for me at the moment, and I have my best interests at heart; I have complete solace. This all sounds beautiful, right? I bet it sounds like I have it all together now, but I don't. This wasn't an overnight process. It took me a complete year to heal and about six years before that to realize I *needed* healing. I'm nowhere near done growing, but I can at least help you get to where I am now.

For starters, there are a few things that you have to realize before stepping into your "season." This is your designated changing station of life. This is the exact space in time of which God has chosen to shift you and the situations around you for your good. In the beginning, you have to accept the fact that no one is obligated to give a damn about you. Stop setting high expectations for people who have no intentions on fulfilling them. It only leaves you disappointed in *them* when you should really be disappointed in yourself for being so naive. Be honest with yourself, you knew who you were dealing with from the beginning yet you're forcing them to be something they don't know how to be. You want to know what you call people like that? They are *seat fillers*. Have you ever watched an award show on television and noticed that all the seats in the audience are full, even though there are clearly people on stage and clearly people accepting awards? Well, those seats are being held by *seat fillers*. Random people being paid to dress up, look important, feel invited and deliver a facade just to give off the impression that things are all together. They fill up empty seats while the person who the seat rightfully belongs to is elsewhere (you can catch that on the way home.) Here's where you work on separating the real from the fake, *accepting* the fakes posing as the real and knowing when it's time for them to get up out that seat!

Secondly, you also have to understand that unfortunate shit will happen to you no matter if you deserve it or not. Bad things happen to good people all the time and bad things happen to bad people just as often. The fact of the matter is, SHIT HAPPENS. You are not exempt from heartache, poverty, sickness or any misfortune just because you do "all the right things." So, kill the dramatics and take life on as it comes full speed. Prepare yourself for battle; if you stay ready, you'll never have to get ready. For years I thought nothing terrible could happen to me without there being a legitimate reason. I had to have fully deserved it, or it made no sense. But what I failed to realize was that not everything is followed by an explanation. Sometimes life just happens and that's as simple as it gets. So stop stressing yourself out looking for the "why" in every situation. Think of it this way, God never said the weapons wouldn't form, He just said that they wouldn't prosper. Let me break that down a little further while trying not to lose you:

A lot of believers sometimes misinterpret scriptures, even the hardcore saints. You'll hear a ton of them constantly telling you how God won't put more on you than you can bare and "No weapon formed against you shall prosper." But, their error occurs once they begin to only use those scriptures as a crutch for every situation they go through without fully understanding its meaning. For example, have you ever notice how as soon as someone goes broke they act as if it "wasn't supposed to happen to them"? As if God made them exempt to trials and tribulations? Then they start quoting scriptures that they've misinterpreted just to help them cope with what's going on around them. What they fail to realize is that in Isaiah 54:17, God isn't saying that bad things won't happen, in fact, He's saying that the weapons ARE INEVITABLE. They *will* come, shit *will* happen and you *will* experience discomfort. But, God is saying that He won't allow them to *win*. They *won't* keep you down; you'll have people out to get you, but they won't get close enough to touch you. You'll go broke, but you won't stay broke. Sickness will come, but healing will follow. *That's* what He meant. So, again, He never said the weapons wouldn't form, He just said they wouldn't prosper.

The next order of business is to claim your destiny before you reach it. Too many of us are waiting until we get to our destiny to start saying it's ours. This is probably the most detrimental thing you can do to yourself while you are on your journey. What you're doing is wondering until you have no choice but to stop. You're lost up until the point where something starts to look a little like where you should be. You have no sense of direction because you haven't even figured out where you're going yet or how you're going to get there. This will only leave you uncomfortable and disappointment because you've started adjusting at the moment you should have already been well settled in. Adjusting comes first; adjust your mind, adjust your spirit, adjust your emotions and be ready to receive what is rightfully yours. Walk by faith and not by sight.

Also, be aware of people that try to school you on how you should move throughout your self-pilgrimage. Do not allow anyone to tell you how to heal. You know what is best for you so do what is best for you, only. Fuck who gets mad at the fact that you've "changed." You're damn right I've changed! Why in the hell would I want to remain stagnant? In the words of Kevin Hart, for anyone who feels the need to tell you about yourself, you tell *them* that I told *you* to tell *them* to "mind their, gotdamned, muthafuckin business, bitch." Period.

I cannot tell you how many people have tried telling me how to take care of myself. Especially, from those that are older and, seemingly, wiser. But, they don't have all the answers. I got this.

That probably ruffled a few feathers, but that in itself also ruffles a few fucks that I do not give. This is real. This is what no one is willing to let you know. Everyone is telling you to "stay strong" and "keep going" but they never include the instruction manual. You may be asking yourself, "what does staying strong intel?", "what and who am I going to have to let go of in order to keep going?". The truth of the matter is that every win comes with its losses. I've let a handful of people go without giving them a notice, not entirely out of pettiness but mostly because I hadn't fully grasped why God was telling me to cut them loose just yet. A few of you may be hesitating to remove certain people out of your life because you've been conditioned to believe you need them there. They are either taking care of you financially, materialistically or sexually and you're afraid that if you let them go, you will lack in said areas. Personally, God has never taken anything away from me without sliding through with the upgrade, so let Him help you make room for better.

On the other end of the spectrum, some of you won't cut people off because you don't want to create drama. It's some real emotional and entitled ass people in the world who feel as though you're wrong for getting rid of them or changing their role in your life. Those people are the selfish type so please let their asses go, immediately. You don't have to beef with a muthafucka after you've cut them off and if that's the case then maybe you need to check yourself. There's a certain level of maturity you have to have while being on the giving and receiving end of a "cut off." You have to be mature enough to let go and mature enough to accept the fact that *yo* ass gotta go! If you see me in public after that and it's an issue, you're going to be standing there looking like "booboo" and "the fool" because I will not entertain foolishness. It is very possible to separate and remain cordial; I don't hate you, I just can't fuck with you.

What you're afraid to let go of is usually what's holding you back, baby, so just leave all them muthafucka's behind. It's okay to cut ties with that girlfriend if you don't think she's as solid as she claims to be, it's okay to block shorty's number and all of his social media accounts. You will have some fallouts with your family from time to time. Sometimes that "friend" you need to cut off ends up being your cousin, sister, brother, mom or dad. Yes, you're going to cry a lot. No, you're not going to like every decision that you'll have to make. No, everyone may not be rooting you on and yes, your faith will be tested and you'll question your spirituality. A lot of this you will do on your own and that's just fine because it'll all be worth it in the end. These things will come to look and feel like huge [L]osses, but what helped me was a simple change of perspective.

I am currently accepting every [L] that I face: [L]essons, they are learned through experience and cannot be taught by telling, only by doing. [L]ove, it comes from friends who know how to be friends, from family and most importantly from myself. I even accept the lack of love I've received from these little brown boys because shit happens. [Lies], something that everyone seems to be doing more often than usual. I accept being [L]eft and trusting that I'll be alright. Feeling [L]ost and understanding that I'm only twenty-one and probably won't have shit together at twenty-two. [L]onliness, with this comes solitude and seclusion and they have become my best friends, I have no need for extra company. [L]aziness, it's a curse but I eventually get off my ass and that's all that matters. [L]ight, figuratively and literally, it's great for your skin and even better for spirit lifting. [L]aughter, I do a lot of that! [L]ackluster, a come and go feeling, but when it leaves my comebacks are killer! So, with all that being said, not once will you hear me mention a loss from this moment forward. I do not take losses. We are all a mess, but we are all blessed. So remind yourselves of this in private and in public. Talk to your inner self and tell them they're doing a great job so far, then tap the next person on the shoulder and tell them the same thing.

2. CHESS NOT CHECKERS

"A man has always wanted to lay me down, but he has never wanted to pick me up." — Eartha Kitt

So, here's where I let you all up in my business. This is where the tea starts spilling over into everyone's cups. Since I've been mouthing away about all of these experiences I've had, I might as well fill you in, right? Here it goes.

Lesson #1: When it Comes Down to Love and Relationships, Play Chess, not Checkers.

The first thing I realized once I started dating was that I've always been the smartest one in the relationship as far as common sense. No matter how smart of a guy

I've dated, they have always done something stupid or said something just as ignorant.

Unfortunately, the type of men I prefer aren't always the best ones for me. I didn't have a man in my life that I expected the men that pursued me to mirror. My daddy was a provider for my mother, financially. But, he seemed very absent from her emotionally. At times he seemed cold, negligent of her needs, and disrespectful out of irritation from areas in which she may have lacked as a wife. I never saw how my grandfather's interacted with my grandmothers, they slept in separate rooms. My boy cousins were all older and had girlfriends and baby mamas back to back. Basically, the men in my family weren't the best when it came to being great men towards the women they were intimate with. This didn't make any of them bad people, they just weren't that good at loving. However, they treated the women in their family's like queens. My father gave me flowers, took me out to eat at nice restaurants, bought me jewelry, held doors open for me, and schooled me on these little brown boys at a very young age. But, as far as what to look for in a significant other, the men in my family only showed me examples of what I didn't want from a man. I saw what I did want from movies, TV shows, and books. That's how I molded the type of man I wanted.

I liked bad guys with good hearts—it sounds even worse when I say this aloud. Let me break it down for you. I love a multifaceted, "hood nigga." That's the type of guy that can indulge in a good book and educate me on street etiquette. His playlist ranges from the rawest, neo-soul to the realest street shit. He loves museums and playing spades. He's book and street smart. His idea of romance is a candlelit dinner, some dark liquor, a backwood and a succulent 6pc with extra mild sauce. He wants to hear spoken word but he totes guns that talk nicely too. Yea, he probably used to crack cards but he's pursuing a career as an investment banker now. But realistically, this man does not exist, which would explain my failed relationships.

Now, don't get me wrong, I've dealt with other types of dudes besides "hood niggas." I even fell in love with a couple of them. I fell in love with their potential and exhausted the possibilities of everything we could've become for one another. These young men had every opportunity to become what I needed of them and were fully equipped to do so, it was all just a matter of timing. Timing that involved me mostly waiting and them mostly wasting, but I'm a strong believer in chance and an even stronger believer in love.

I started dating when I was fourteen, simultaneously fell in love for the first time and, inconveniently, had my first heartbreak. In love at fourteen? Absolutely. This wasn't puppy love, lust, fascination or a fixation. I was wholeheartedly in love with this young man. How did I know I was in love and didn't just have a love for him? Let me break it down for you: When you simply love someone you care about them, you enjoy their company and you're connected emotionally. Everything they do or say affects you immensely; their opinions matter. They are your "person." They are your "LOVE-friend", as I like to term it. Once you end things, however, there's an emotional disconnect. What they do after you no longer matters, you wish them well but aren't bothered if "well" doesn't necessarily occur for them. They are past tense. When you're in love, this person is an extraction of everything that you are. They are your peace and vice versa, they mirror all of your flaws and insecurities in the purest and healthiest way. You care about them beyond just their well being— how's their mental and emotional health? Did they pray today? Why have they been gaining or losing weight? What's their thought process like?

To love is to feel whole; you feel safe in the fact that you have someone. To be in love is to feel complete, meaning no pieces are missing. They're not opposite, they're just on different realms. Once you end things with someone you're in love with, they don't become past tense, they're just repositioned. They're not depleted, they're just no longer in the forefront of your life. "I love you, but I can live without you." versus " I'm in love with you, I can live without you… but I'd rather not."

So with that being said, yes, I fell in love at fourteen. But, like everything else in life, falling in love doesn't come with an instruction manual. I knew what I was feeling but I didn't know how to deal with those feelings effectively, he and I were both lost. He quickly became one of my first examples of what not to look for in a man. Sidenote, for any mad bitch or sad bitch reading this that are expecting me to bad mouth this young man, just skip these next few paragraphs because that's not my steelo. I will not bash him, and I will not throw dirt on his name, I will not belittle him, I will not make him out to be the worst person in the world. But I will speak my truth and say he did a terrible job of taking care of my heart and respecting the love that I gave him. That is not a feeling, that is a fact. For five years, on and off, I allowed someone I loved to cheat, lie and manipulate me at his will. Do I have any doubt about him loving me? Absolutely not. He wanted to love me the right way but he was just incapable. Remember what I said about having high expectations for people who you know will only end up letting you down? That was the case here. I knew he was lying and cheating, I knew he wasn't supposed to be disrespecting me the way that he was, I knew he never wanted a future with me, yet I still convinced myself that it was all in my head. This was the dumbest shit I could've done to myself. He was the first man I allowed to hurt me, back to back, with no repercussions; he had nothing to lose. He took advantage of the fact that I loved him more than I loved myself, therefore he was my vessel. I fed off his presence in order to survive, figuratively speaking. We met during the most trying years of my life and it felt as if he was the only thing going well for me, he was the only thing that made sense.

Unfortunately, it took me five years to consider myself and my feelings in that situation. I was hurt and bitter for a long time, and I hated him for being so careless with my heart and not being apologetic about it. I felt he owed me his muthafuckin' life! But after about a year I came to realize that hating him forever was only going to hurt me even more, so I forgave him for myself and moved on. Just like bad things happen to good people, good people do bad things. It doesn't necessarily make them bad people, it just makes them human. This guy was a great person. He had a huge heart, loved the shit out of his family, did whatever he could to help the people around him, gave his last if he could and loved kids. He had great qualities, he was in touch with his emotions, he didn't play about his education, he was business driven and money motivated. He loved God, prayed all the time and embraced his spirituality. The only problem was him not knowing how to love me correctly. Eventually, he did become capable of loving a woman and has since then had a child. And guess what? I'm happier for him than I've ever been. With a heart like mine, I don't know how to shut my love off and on when a situation turns hot or cold. I've always wanted the best for him, and I've always wanted him to be happy, even if it wasn't with me. That's real.

Throughout the five years I invested into this guy I learned two very important things as a woman: know you're worth and never settle. It takes energy to love another person. That energy has to stem from your psyche: mind, soul, and spirit. But, before you can offer all of those things up to the next person, you have to surrender those things to yourself. Love inwardly, first, and outwardly, second. You cannot pour from an empty cup and you cannot prepare a meal with an empty fridge. Stock your fridge with self-reassurance, self-preservation, self-care, self-love and self-acceptance and then feed your guests. If they aren't satisfied, send them on their way but don't let your food go to waste. Either feed into yourself or find someone who doesn't just eat to get full, but eats for nourishment. You are pepper steak and rice, not top ramen. Know your worth. Never settle. This one's for y'all too, fellas!

After the first heartbreak, the rest never get any easier, you just get a lot smarter. I started learning from my mistakes and the mistakes of my partners and began to move more strategically. I chose my interests based off of criteria. I became more attentive and more alert. I played my life like a game of chess, not checkers. The game of chess involves patience and preparation. Each piece on the board has a specific job, each piece works together to fulfill it. As opposed to chess, checkers is less intense, less demanding and doesn't require too much attention. Are you following me? I started taking my needs a lot more seriously and began learning more about what I expected of myself in a relationship and not just my partner. Am I a pro at relationships now? Hell no. But I am more experienced, allowing me to make fewer and fewer mistakes.

I've been fortunate enough to have great loves and unfortunate enough to have the worst. I've had genuine relations and copycat affiliates. I've literally had the best and worst all in a span of seven years. Some of these experiences were first hand, others I experienced from the outside looking in. I've observed just as many successful and failed relationships as I have been in, if not more. However, in year twenty-one I never expected to encounter, not one, but three heartbreaks from three very different young men.

Again, my first love was at the mere age of fourteen but my best love came to me at age twenty. It was the best love I've ever been gifted to receive in all of my years of being in relationships. He was the most caring, sensitive, understanding person I'd ever met! This boy loved me better than I loved myself at that moment and I loved him just as much. At first sight, it was more like a soul recognition. Almost as if our hearts had been beating apart for so long until our rhythms finally met; everything was in sync. To be honest, we were perfect. Everyone supported our relationship. My parents loved him, he met my WHOLE DAMN FAMILY. This muthafucka was the one, okay? It wasn't until rumors of him being unfaithful traveled back to me that we started having issues. There was a shift, an odd shift, but a shift, nevertheless. I don't think either one of us knew how to handle it so we just parted ways. I can't quite put my finger on it, but something was causing a disconnect, and for two people who had been connected emotionally, mentally and spiritually for almost a year, it scared the fuck out of both of us. He stopped picking up my phone calls and leaving my messages on delivered. The times I was able to get through to him he'd sit on the phone and ignore me or hang up to finish "kickin' it" with his boys."Although we felt perfect, he still had his flaws and as in love with him as I was, I wasn't going to ignore them. We drifted apart emotionally, then physically and now we don't speak at all. Yet, our love for one another remains & his name forever remains in my prayers. However, he needs to continue to stay the fuck away from me. I have no intentions on rekindling any flame that has fled.

Though this may have been my best love, it wasn't my worst heartbreak, that came about a month or so after. Now, I bet you're like, "Bitch, you bounce back fast as hell!" but this love wasn't new, it had manifested since I was thirteen years old. I made one of the best friends a girl could have at a somewhat young age. We were fuckin' inseparable! Whatever I needed, emotionally, he took care of that. Wherever I lacked intellectually, he corrected me and vice versa. He was my confidant, my protector, my homie, my prayer partner and eventually became one of the best loves of my life. But this was one of those friendships that should have never crossed over into the territory. What we saw as "destiny" really turned out to be a disaster. On my end, I fell for the okie doke; I allowed my love for a man to cloud my judgment as a woman. I let him make promises he couldn't keep, which never happened until we pushed for something deeper and I allowed myself to play a role that was way out of my character. This was one of those inopportune loves— a love that time had no room or space for, yet we pushed for it, foolishly. This was the first time he and I didn't bounce back from our differences and I ended up losing my best friend in the whole world and the rawest love I've ever felt. People think a break up is the worst, on the contrary, it is ending a friendship that has the hardest hit. Therefore, imagine what it was like to lose both. I couldn't call my best friend and cry it out because that was him. I couldn't call my best friend and ask for advice because that was him— I lost so much in one person. You never really get over shit like that, you just learn to accept it for what it is.

Now, try and stay with me because this last love lost is going to tie all of this together and the message will soon come. This heartbreak was the most pivotal. This love story brewed the quickest but was just as hot and strong. Remember how I mentioned I had a "type"? Well, this wasn't quite it but it was a close enough settlement I was willing to make. This young man was like my trouble child, the one that needed mothers love the most but was too stubborn and naive to realize it. He came to me fucked up already, but it was still so much beauty in what was broken that I stuck around. He was cold most times but had a smile that could warm anyone's heart. He was mean but I had witnessed him do so many things out of the kindness of his heart. He lied, cheated and stole, but he was still pure & I loved him to his core (and I still do.). Despite our pains, we were absolutely in love. But in the beginning, his love hurt. I had never been disrespected, neglected nor rejected as often by any man until I met him. At the start of our relationship, he pushed me to tears every other day and it felt as if he wasn't the least bit apologetic. He was the first man to ever call me out of my name, and still, I stayed. He was never abusive physically but could tear a wall down with his words. Being as hypersensitive as I am, this was the most dangerous situation I could've been in. He cared way more about his comfort and wellbeing than mine. He embarrassed me countless times & allowed for me to look exactly how he'd made me feel: like a goofy. In addition to my struggle with anxiety and depression, this companionship nearly destroyed me.

However, he still found ways to make me love him more each day. There's no laugh as soul-satisfying as his and there's no embrace as heartwarming as his. Despite his ugly ways, he is love in its most vulnerable state. But sooner enough he did what every other man had done to me, and that was abandoning me. He left me at my lowest point, even being part of the reason why I had become so low. He ended things in a text, blocked me and left me fucked up! I drank myself to sleep every night for three weeks. I had a shot of whiskey every morning and drank up until my sleep took me out. I skipped so many classes, spent seventy-five percent of my days drunk and crying, stopped speaking to everyone— I was sunken. I felt that if it was this easy for these guys to leave me, then I must not be worth keeping. Then one day, I woke up and for the first time in weeks, I didn't want to drink. I was sad still but couldn't push myself to cry anymore. So, I started praying: I promised God I'd seek solace in him before seeking it in man. I asked him for peace and contentment and to make me anew. The next day I went to my third counseling session, threw away all the liquor I had left, made a list of things I sought out in life and got my shit together. I now pray every day all day and spread as much comfort and love as I can because I know it'll come back tenfold. I am mentally, emotionally and spiritually stable and all it took was a full-blown breakdown. But that situation was my biggest blessing in disguise. I once read somewhere that you've never truly loved someone until you've prayed to God to give you the strength to let them go—and man did I pray. But no matter the extent of pain I felt, the love I had for him— The love we had for each other, overpowered all of the bullshit I had endured.

He's the first person I ever truly put work into being with and vice versa. You give a man time without you, and he'll realize you're presence is way more comfortable than your absence. So to that young man, thank you. I don't fault you for your ill ways because I see you from the inside out, not the outside in. You are beautiful regardless of how damaged you may appear. There's no hate in my heart for you, in fact, I love you more today than I ever have. Though I have no ill feelings towards you, I am very disappointed in how you chose to handle me. I gave you my best parts and you took advantage— shame on you. All in all, Keep your head up, keep God first, but most importantly, keep healing.

So, here's the lesson within the message: Experience love in as many ways as you can. Heal at your own pace and on your own terms. Lastly, encourage yourself to forgive. Consider your self worth at all times. Young women, especially black women, are always deemed "too complicated" and "too picky" when it comes to choosing a man. Sadly, most of this commentary comes from the black men that we call son, brother, and father. One of my favorite female rappers, Destiny Frasqueri, aka Princess Nokia, gave her opinion on the "angry black woman" stigma in an interview with VFiles "How To Be A Bitch 101":

"I think a lot of people assume that brown women are angry and coarse, but, I think that we rightfully are so. I don't give a fuck any-fucking-more... I have a high caliber for what I find acceptable."

BE LIKE PRINCESS NOKIA. So what, if a man thinks you're standards and qualifications for him are outrageous or unattainable? Thank him, actually, because that's one less man you have to waste your time on. This goes for both women and men. Fellas, if a girl does not meet your expectations as the woman of your liking, move her along. Men want things that go beyond looks as well and what a lot of us fail to understand is that you can't expect anything from a companion that you don't even bring to the table. Jot that down. You want me to be financially stable, educated, romantic and sexually fulfilling? Cool. But can you balance a checkbook, recommend a good novel for me to read, surprise me with candlelit dinners and sex me well on the regular? If the answer is no then you probably need to meet your expectations at eye level, because that's where you'll find the one for you.

Just remember that love is timeless, it'll never expire or run out. Therefore you have no need to rush to or through it. As much as people want to believe it, love is not something you chase, it's something you meet. All the fairytales have us fucked up out here thinking Prince Charming is on his way to find us while we sit still and wait, or that your queen is busy knocking out peasants and pleasers until she finally gets to you and realizes "you're the one." Love is not planned, forced, foreseen or expected. Love is sporadic and unscripted, you almost never see it coming. But once it meets you, you know exactly what it is. It is the only thing you can be familiar with without it having ever been seen. Remember, this is chess. Practice patience and preparation. You don't always have to be on the lookout for love, but just make sure you're ready to receive it when you meet it.

1 Corinthians 13:4-8 New International Version (NIV)
4 Love is patient, love is kind. It does not envy, it does not boast, it is not proud. 5 It does not dishonor others, it is not self-seeking, it is not easily angered, it keeps no record of wrongs. 6 Love does not delight in evil but rejoices with the truth. 7 It always protects, always trusts, always hopes, always perseveres.

8 Love never fails. But where there are prophecies,

they will cease; where there are tongues, they will be stilled; where there is knowledge, it will pass away.

3. DON'T TAKE IT PERSONAL

1 CORINTHIANS 15:33 DO NOT BE MISLED: "BAD COMPANY CORRUPTS GOOD CHARACTER."

My condolences to anyone who has ever lost me
And, to anyone who got lost in me
Or, to anyone who ever felt they took a loss
with me
My apologies for the misunderstanding or the
lack thereof
I'm sorry you missed the God in me
And I'm sorry you missed the light
I'm sorry you forgot the way I arose like the
moon
Night after night with the burden to forgive
Eager to feed you everything

See, I'm a holy woman
I know what it's like to give life to a being
without ever needing to press skin against one
another
I've practiced how to hold my tongue long enough
I'm afraid I forgot to say goodbye
I'm afraid you're under the impression
That I was made to please you
I was under the impression you understood me
better
The truth is, I'm a superwoman
And some days I'm an angry woman
And some days I'm a crazy woman
For still waiting, for still loving harder even if
I'm aching
For still trusting that I'm still worth the most
For still searching for someone to understand
me better
—Reyna Biddy

There's always that one muthafucka that's telling you how you've changed as if it's the worst thing you could've done for yourself. Or, the "friend" that's genuinely bothered by your growth because it's, in turn, separating you from them. Then, there's the asshole who feels as though you need to "humble yourself" because you're "doing too much" or "dreaming too big." To be honest, all three of them muthafuckas can eat a thick dick. Anyone who claims to be your friend should never encourage you to stunt your growth to make them more comfortable. If anything, they should be pushing you past your expectations, praying for your success and not preying on your downfall. Jot that down. Beware of those people's intentions. They are experts in the act of fraudulence. You'll think they're rooting for you, but they're really just trying to remain relevant so that they can say "I was there" in case you make it. Remember what I said about seat fillers? This is a prime example of someone taking up a seat that is not rightfully theirs. Here's some advice: Tell them to get the fuck up and allow the right person to be seated. Fuck who it rubs the wrong way, fuck who it hurts and fuck who's not in agreeance. If it's the best decision for you to move forward in the healthiest way, do that shit. I remember watching this video of Judge Lynn speaking to this young woman about the importance of year twenty and this is what she said:

"Twenty is for you, twenty is for growth, twenty is for the pursuit of a tomorrow that is better than today, twenty is for options, twenty is for passion and knowledge and enjoyment. It is not for continuous compromise… twenty

is opportunity to move onward, upward and forward.
Get a large life…"

LISTEN TO JUDGE LYNN. This is some of the best advice a person can receive when living out their twenties. Stay far away from compromise and never settle for anything or anyone in life. God has never taken anything from me without sliding through with an upgrade. Therefore, let go of what and who needs to be let go of so that you can make room for the upgrade. Ask anyone that knows me well enough and they'll be sure to tell you, "Mimi is quick to cut a muthafucka loose." Some see this as unhealthy, but I learned early on how to master not giving a fuck about anyone's opinion of my life decisions. The moment my discernment tells me, "that muthafucka gotta go, sis", the scissors are coming out.

Baby, let me tell you something, the fact that someone doesn't belong in your life does not have to be taken personally. Sometimes, people and things just don't belong. I don't have to hate you after I cut you off, I'll just no longer allow you to play a role that was never meant for you. It's very immature and foolish to be offended by someone choosing to remove you from their life for their betterment, especially if there is legit reasoning. It only becomes offensive once you stop fucking with people who have elevated you and carefully invested in your life, without any real reason. I've been on both ends so I can speak on this, and I've accepted the outcome in both situations.

I've been let go of and I've done the letting go, both times I accepted the reasons for what they were, even if there were no reasons at all. That's called maturity.

Though cutting people off doesn't come too hard for me, I find it most difficult to cut ties with family members. Does that shock you? You know, the idea of cutting family off just as you would a friend? I'm only asking because I've had a few people frown upon my decision to do so because it "just isn't right". But here's how I see it: A person is a person. I treat everyone the same no matter who they are to me. Wrong is wrong, disrespect is disrespect, and so forth. Therefore, if my mother is toxic to my spiritual, mental and physical maintenance, mama gotta go. If my sister is out to ruin me out of envy and jealousy, sis gotta go. If grandma is talking shit about me to everyone in the family, granny gotta go! Point blank, period. Nobody is safe, baby. I have a spirit to protect at all times, and it is my responsibility to myself to make sure no one tries to tarnish it. Again, it doesn't always have to be taken personally. Cutting your mother off isn't you saying you don't love her, it's you saying that you need to love yourself and rid your environment of anyone and anything who is causing you pain. So, whoever may be judging you right now for making a decision like this, fuck 'em. They're not doing the living for you, you are. This is the most appropriate time to be selfish.

Be selfish with your time, for it is not to be wasted. Be selfish with your love, for it is not to be toyed with. Nurture relationships that act as assets, not liabilities. Jot that down.

For a long while I held on to people simply because I felt as though if I were to let them go, it'd be considered a loss. I didn't want them to go off and find something better than my friendship, love or companionship. I didn't want to hurt them and risk the chances of them liking or accepting me. I didn't want to be alone, had I decided to stop dealing with them. Because of this, I missed out on a ton of opportunities and blessings. But, I remember preparing for the year of 2017 and asking God to give me a sign as to how I should maneuver throughout the year to make sure I didn't shorten myself of any blessings. He sent me the word *release* in a dream. Release all things that have hurt you and run the risk of hurting you, let go of grudges and bitterness, let go of toxic binds, etc. At that moment I vowed 2017 to be my year of release. From that point on God continued to show me that He is more than present at all times. About a week or so after having that dream I began to see that word everywhere I looked. Literally, I could be scrolling on Facebook and see five to ten posts about releasing things in the year of 2017. I'd even come across videos sending out messages about the importance of release and cleansing. But, the clearest sign God gave me was First Sunday service, and I walked in to see a large banner in the pulpit that read: 2017, The Year of Release. I was at a loss for words. How coincidental could it be that the same message God sent me, He had also sent to my congregation? However, I didn't question God. I simply did what He told me to do. I let go of so many things in year twenty-one and I don't regret any decision I made to do so. I let go of self-doubt, fear of change, excuses, bitterness, bad friends, old lovers, mental health neglect, and so much more. Since doing so, I am the best I've ever been and I have so much more left to do.

So, to those that may have gotten dropped along my voyage of self-pilgrimage: Your season had simply ran its course. I held on to you for as long as God had allowed me to do so, but once He told me to *release*, I had to be obedient. Had I kept you around neither of us would've been able to grow. For some of you I may not have given forewarning, and for that I will apologize. But, everything was happening too quickly for me to stop and explain. I wish nothing but the best for you, as I always have. I do not regret my decision, nor will you be welcomed back. However, should you need me, I'll be sure to say a prayer and mention your name twice.

4. BLACK MAN.

This chapter of the book is the only one that required research beyond my knowledge. If I'm not mistaking I'm sure every man reading this is convinced that this is a "woman's book." So, to prove you wrong, I'm dedicating an entire chapter to you. I know a lot about men, but still, that's only a little compared to what they're truly about. First, I'll share with you what I've learned from personal experience. Disclaimer: these are not facts, these are opinions based off of the experiences I've had with the black men in my life:

One
Men are logical thinkers. They are simple and straightforward. Even the deepest of deep, poetic, artistic, man can't tap into his emotions as naturally as a woman. To be honest, we as women cannot fault them for being so... limited. God created Adam to do very

distinct, specific tasks. Adam named each animal on Earth, without hassell. Adam was the first linguist, immediately after his creation he knew words, he formulated clear sentences, he was natural at direct communication. Adam, unlike Eve, was the only one who didn't need to be convinced to eat the forbidden fruit. All it took was an immediate proposition from a woman without any real reasoning. While it took Eve to be persuaded and emotionally enthralled by the devil to give into temptation. These are all examples of man's ability to reason, communicate and make sound decisions. As much as women would love to have a man who can read their mind, pick up on their mood changes, tap into their emotional needs without being told, and knows exactly what to do and say to make a woman feel good on their own… it's damn near impossible. Men are not built that way. If you are upset with a man, he may notice but nine times out of ten he doesn't know why. Tell him. If you're in the mood for romance and want to be wooed and tended to, he could most likely make that happen, but most times you also have to tell him that that's what you want. Speak. If you're feeling as though your man isn't being honest and your relationship is on the line, he could be completely innocent or may need to reveal something to you and doesn't know how, so LET HIM KNOW WHAT THE HELL IS GOING ON IN YOUR HEAD. Are you not being satisfied in bed like you'd like? Tell that man or he's gonna keep rockin' that tired ass boat until you change the wave. As complicated as men seem, they are typically easy to pick apart. They are always predictable, however, it is their cooperation that is mostly out of reach unless this man truly cares and loves you. Other than that, a man is going to act right for whoever he wants to act right for. Period. There is literally no in-betweens when it comes to men. It's either A or B.

Two

Men are prideful. There isn't a man on this earth who thinks he isn't entitled to some sort of respect from people, in general, let alone just women. Very rarely will you meet a man and he's not indirectly arrogant, a physical overachiever or disturbingly accredited. But, they know that even if there's something a woman doesn't like about them, there's always going to be at least one thing she won't be able to stop thinking about. Men are calculated with their cockiness. They know exactly what to say and how to say it (not all men, but we're going to speak for the majority). No matter how sensational women are, we cannot out smooth a man. They believe in their steelo more than they believe in anything else. It takes a savvy woman to humble a man. But we as women have to admit, we're suckas for that shit.

Three

Men love hard. I've seen men display a type of love that I only dream of experiencing before I leave this world. A man loves his mama as if she were God, Himself. He worships everything about her: her cooking, her jokes, her wisdom. Everything. The love and affection they exhibit towards their family and friends is so beautiful. When they have found the woman God has made for them, they give her the world and some. Adoration. Consideration. Motivation. They are all present when a man loves. They love as though they'll never get it again. Disclaimer: *Man* is not equivalent to any male with a penis. Everything I just described are qualities that are of a MAN. A mature, wise, individual. You little boys cannot relate. But, I digress.

Four

You cannot change a man. Once a man is set in his ways there is no convincing him that he needs to do things differently than he has been doing them for years. As a woman, you're only going to end up hurting yourself and driving a man away. A man is going to love you the way he wants to love you. The right man will love you how you need to be loved. K. Michelle said it best, "you can't raise a man." Either accept them or find what you want elsewhere.

Now, as I mentioned before, there is so much I cannot explain about a man because I simply don't know.

However, to make sure I did this chapter justice, I have turned to a handful of the black men in my life for some guidance. I based my research off of four common questions black women had for black men.

What does it take for a man to tap into his emotions? And not just express sadness or empathy or sympathy, but actually let your guards down and connect with a companion or even a friend. Why are men so apprehensive to doing so even if they know it'll better your situations with your sig other or friend?

Why do men feel the need to keep ahold of certain women in their lives who they need to let go of for the betterment of the WOMAN? Honestly. *Why you bother us when you know you don't want us? Why you bother us when you know you got a woman? Why you bother us when you know you know better?*

In what ways is your masculinity tested? In other words, what do you avoid doing and saying as a man to avoid seeming "gay" or "soft"? This can be in terms of relationships or friendships with women.

What do you want women to understand that you think we will never tap into? It can be anything.

So, black men… here's to your proverb.

hypermasculinity: the exaggeration of male stereotypical behaviour, such as an emphasis on physical strength, aggression, and sexuality.

So when does it become *"toxic"* for black men?

Black men are conditioned from a very young age to carry themselves a certain way: Be strong both physically and emotionally, if you cry you're weak, if you show your feelings you're too vulnerable, don't "act gay", act cool so you can get all the girls, be tough, not tender. Being bigger and better is the goal of being a man and if you fail to meet the expectations then you've initially failed as a man. It seems as though the only way to be considered a man is to overextend your masculinity.

Though much of this is a dependant upon how one is raised, a lot of it could also be embedded while a man is in the midst of learning to love a woman or experiencing some of the lowest points of his life. When a man loves a woman, I mean genuinely loves a woman, he enters a different realm of manhood. At this point he has a responsibility to another person's feelings, heart, body, spirit, and soul. When a man loses something or faces defeat, he has no choice but to expose himself emotionally in order for him to grow and recuperate.

Unfortunately, anything that promotes vulnerability from a black man is frowned upon by public societies and private societies— family. Depending on the type of man he already is determines how much work needs to go into reaching the core of the many layers that are him— how deep do we have to dig?

Let's ask ourselves: What separates a black man from any other man on earth? Their essence. The essence of a black man runs much deeper than physical strength. It's made up of much more than muscle, stamina and facial hair. It is coated in pure blackness. However, though that blackness is beautiful, it is also dangerous— inwardly and outwardly. A black man deals with much more than the average man: lack of employment, bias, lack of educational resources, judgment and ridicule, hate and violence, expectancy to be a provider, etc. A black man has to conquer all of those things in order to be considered a MAN… in order to be acknowledged as a man of productivity. That's some stressful shit. Therefore as a black woman you have to be aware of the struggles that your black man may bring to your attention and those that you may know nothing about. Again, men are not open to showing weakness. A man could lose his job but will not show his friends and family his panic nor his disappointment. A man could be struggling financially, but he'll never show anyone his pockets and admit he's fucked up. A man can lose his woman and be dying inside, but he'll never reveal that to his boys. I can only imagine how lonely that may feel. How tough life may seem. How desperate you may be. From very young ages you've been conditioned to look differently than you feel. And what's even more disappointing is that most of the ridicule you receive comes from other black men. The very ones who are supposed to empathize with you, are giving you the most grief! But, as a growing young woman, I get it now. Just as us women feel misunderstood, we have to understand that our young men are just as unseen.

A man may come across as heartless when he's absent towards certain emotions. He may seem weak because he's too aware of his emotions. He may appear cocky when really he's just been taught to always come out on top because that's what's expected of a man. He may look like a "bitch" for his lack of aggressiveness. Here's where things become toxic. Let's use relationships as an example: If a black man were to show the slightest amount of unprecedented affection towards his significant other, oddly enough he feels as though he's lessened his value as a man. His biggest problems stem from pride and ego; men are praised for how many women they can have. If you can pull girls you're "cool". Do you get hoes? Ok, you're "cool." Men are taught to conquer women from a very young age. They are taught to get to and through as many as you can, leaving no time for permanent affection. The woman that can keep your attention long enough to establish some sort of emotional attachment, is the one. Until then, however, "have your fun." Unfortunately, black men find that woman and still don't know how to tap into his emotions no matter how strong his love is for her. Sometimes it's due to stubbornness and immaturity, but other times it's simply because they don't know how. Because we black women have been conditioned to be nurturing creatures, we are easily irritable towards our men when they struggle to show affection, tenderness, consideration, or love. That frustration causes conflict; conflict pushes men away. Once a man is absent physically, a woman is absent emotionally. When a man doesn't receive proper care from his woman, he seeks it elsewhere—from people or things, neither of which are healthy for him. Once he neglects his woman and responsibilities to her, she loses interest and regains independence. Though stubborn, a man knows when he has a good woman, whether he deserves her or not. What he won't do is let a good woman leave, if he's smart. As selfish as it may seem, it's the reality of it all. A man will keep a good thing even if he's the worst thing for her, because he knows she's what he needs.

At the same time, a black man needs to feel needed at all times. He needs to know that he is adding something to you and improving your life in some way. If he isn't, he doesn't feel adequate enough as a man. However, most black women are very independent, especially in this generation. We do for ourselves when it comes to everything, now of days. So we fail in letting a man feel like a man because we feel like less of a strong, black woman. We fail to understand that having a strong woman doesn't make you a weak man and having a strong man doesn't make you less of an independent woman.

Though this isn't everything that comes with being a black man, I hope it sums it up quite well. But to be sure that I've done my part in getting the attention of those in need of this chapter, I'm going to get a little more direct.

To the black man that is headed down a slippery slope of bad company, bad decisions, bad encounters, and bad thoughts: be aware of the liabilities and the assets in your life. Risk should not be the *only* option you have. Discomfort should not be the only feeling you are familiar with. Fear should not dictate your future. Do yourself a favor and set yourself up for greatness. Breaking bad habits is the least easiest thing to do, but, with discipline and encouragement *it gets done!* You're routine only seems comfortable because it is familiar *not* because it is for you. As a young black man in America you were born with a social deficit. You were already defined to this world as a threat, a risk, a liability, an upset, an issue, an underestimation, a loser, a complication— you were already checked off of someone's list! So be mindful of the actions you take because they will either add to or subtract from that definition. There is an entire community of people desperately rooting for you. A community too large to know each individual. So do us a favor and be the best version of yourself that you can possibly be. The only excuse you should ever have is that death took you before you could be who you were suppose to be. So until then, break the cycle of cannot's and could not's. You don't exist there.

To the black man who is struggling with his sexuality: it is a dangerous time for you to be existing in. However, do not let fear keep you from feeling. Above all things, God wants us to be happy. He wants us to seek positive fulfillment. He wants us to have love. Judgment is inevitable. It is inescapable. Hell, they judged Jesus! Give yourself the chance to live before you've decided you've lost. But, be careful. This is a cruel world. An inexplicably cruel world where people are more terrified of gay than they are Trump! Take care of yourself. Move peacefully but not silently. Speak your truths, but don't put yourself in harms way. It is better to live honestly and be hated than to live a lie and be loved.

To the black man that won't accept or acknowledge his *blackness*: Get it together, sweetie. You are who are for a reason. Yes, it is scary to be you.

You're targeted 24/7, you're hated for the most ignorant reasons, you're offered less than the melanin deficient, and it's tough. But do not deny your blackness. Embrace it. It is the sweetest thing this earth has ever grown and that God has ever planted. Instead of letting your blackness work against you, work with it. Your voice echoes even in whispers, black boy. Your skin feeds off of the main light source this universe thrives off of. Do you know who you are? Well, start learning. The world is already against you, the least you can do is be on your own side.

To the black man who has been hurt by a black man: I'm sorry. I hate the man that hurt you. He had no right to take your strength away from you like that. But, forgive him for he, too, had been hurting. Do not let his ill ways keep you from growing and healing. The only thing more harmful than an ignorant black man is a damaged one. You didn't deserve what you were dealt, but you also don't deserve what are allowing the situation to do to you. You are not less of a man. You are not weak. You are not beneath anyone. You are simply scarred. The good thing about scars is that they heal with the proper care. Take note of what you need in this moment and go get it. You are hurting, you are *not* broken.

To the black man raising another black man: do your job. You are the first teacher that they have, perfect your lesson plan as best you can. Love on them! Kiss on them! Hold their hands! Hug them! You're their daddy, you can do that. Practice healthy discipline and explain to them why they're wrong. Allow them to ask questions. Teach them that they can be just as strong and manly with a kind heart. Never abandon them. Be the example you never had and better than the one you did have.

Black man, I hear you. I see you. On behalf of the black woman, we're trying to understand you.

5. SOME SAD SH*T

I'll be the first to admit, I used to be one
ignorant, naive muthafucka. I mean, even now I'm not
the sharpest needle in the bunch, but not too long ago I
was detrimental to myself. I thought I knew everything
and could figure everything out on my own— wrong!
Here's the thing, I grew up as an only child, therefore the
urge for independence had already nested within me
before I actually had any. I wanted to walk to the store
alone, I wanted to make my own money, I wanted to
cook my own food, I wanted to have my own phone, I
wanted to stay home alone, I wanted to go out with my
friends without a chaperone— all of that. However, I
have some extremely overprotective parents. Protective
is one thing, but let's just say, I'm twenty-one now and
they still don't allow me walking to the store alone. I
understand parenting doesn't come with an instruction
manual, and we live in a very dangerous city, but there

comes a point where they have to realize I'm grown and very knowledgeable. It sometimes feels as though they're waiting for me to be perfect before letting me off this leash. They've taught me SO much! I'm wise far beyond my years mostly because of them— watching what they say and what they do. But fear keeps them from trusting their own work of art in the hands of someone else. I do not fault them for anything, however, an explanation behind their commands would help me understand their point of view from time to time. But, I digress.

Being independent means everything to me. I love being able to say I did something on my own. I love being my own BAUCE, and I'm proud to be able to say that I'm the owner of my own business and ambassador of my own brand, today. I make my own money (as best I can without a little help from my parents) and spend it at my leisure. I recently made a vow to myself that I'd explore every one of my talents to the fullest. There's a quote by Erma Bombeck, and it reads, "When I stand before God at the end of my life, I hope that I will have not a single bit of talent left and can say 'I used everything You gave me'." I've made a promise to myself and God to be everything that He has written for me to be. Every day I work on a different craft and every day I'm asking God to instill in me every ounce of motivation I may need in order to come out successful in all of my endeavors. All of my life I've struggled to accept who I am and have been insecure about myself in almost every aspect. I never considered myself pretty, I never felt as if I was as good of a singer as people would claim me to be, I never thought I was as good of an artist as others, I never thought I could dress as well as I was praised for, I never thought I was as smart as my grades reflected, etc. I lived a large portion of my life thinking I wasn't enough. Therefore, I yearned for independence so that I could separate myself from any attachment I may have had to people's opinions of me, their judgment, negativity and so on. Unfortunately, it took awhile for me to gain that independence and in the midst of waiting for it, I allowed a handful of things to discourage and distract me. For one, I was misguided on what I expected independence to do for me; I gave it a task it was never meant to perform. I wanted it to heal me. I wanted it to change minds, I wanted it to alter opinions— I wanted it to do things only God could do. I thought that if I were to have complete control over everything in my life, it'd automatically improve. Therefore, a lot of what I did resulted in disappointment because my expectations of independence were never met and I was never satisfied. This then led to me having a lot of bottled up anger and resentment. I was angry and frustrated all the time with everything and everyone, especially my parents. I felt as if they were the main ones holding me back from my freedom, from my happiness and from my peace. Why couldn't they trust me enough to be my own person and not categorize it as "acting grown" or undermining their authority? Yet again, I digress. All of this eventually led to me sinking into a deep state of depression. In the beginning, I wasn't sure how to label the emotional and psychological discomfort that I was feeling, but as I grew older it was clear that I'd been depressed all those years. I wasn't just "sad", I didn't just "have an attitude", I wasn't just "mean", I was sick— I was not okay. Though this illness rooted from one thing, everything that followed made it worse.

deep breath

I had my first suicidal thought at the age of fourteen. I can't exactly say it was an attempt because I never followed through. I cannot remember what triggered me I just remember being tired. I was drained, I was at my wits end with everything and everyone. I sat in the middle of the kitchen of our apartment with a knife in hand. I remember having the hardest time deciding whether to cut at my wrist first or just stab myself in the stomach and get it over with. I must've sat there and cried for about an hour before my younger cousin that we'd taken in, walked in on me. I didn't move or hide what I was doing and she didn't speak on what she was seeing. She walked over to me, sat down and leaned me over into her lap to lay— She was nine and somehow knew exactly what I needed. I had no one to talk to and quite frankly, I didn't want to talk to anyone about what was going on with me out of fear that they'd judge or wouldn't understand. How can you explain something that you, yourself aren't sure of? I didn't know why my mind convinced me that I was worthless, or that something was always wrong, or that I was at fault for everything that was happening around me. I can't put into words why I cried myself to sleep almost every night for years— silent cries. The cries that you didn't want anyone to hear because you didn't feel like explaining. I couldn't breathe from covering my nose and my mouth so that I wouldn't wake my parents while at home, or wake my roommates while in my dorm at school.

My faith in God was weary. I didn't believe He could do anything good for me, but somehow found ways to do everything good for everyone else *but* me. He and I were strangers for about a year. I didn't care to pray because what the fuck had it done for me thus far? I didn't care for church (nor did I give a damn about the sheisty muthafuckas in the church) because I didn't think God cared for me.

Do you know how empty that feels? To have the one person in the universe you have to depend on become the last person you can depend on. But, just because my praise lacked didn't mean His power did. I was just in a really dark place.

About a year or two after realizing my depression, I began to realize I was also suffering from anxiety. I had my first anxiety attack my freshman year of high school. It was the scariest thing I had ever experienced and it wasn't my last. I've, since then, had about ten attacks and neither of them was easier than the one that came before it because they were all so different. So many people categorize anxiety as nervousness & they stop there. But you want to know what anxiety feels like? It's constantly being concerned about the way you talk and if every word is coming out right, out of fear of looking dumb. Rewinding and replaying old embarrassing moments from years ago and cringing as if it just happened. Walking into a room full of people and tiring yourself in the thought of who's looking at you, for what reason and whether or not you should react or run. Anxiety is worrying about every little thing in life, it goes way past nervousness & overthinking. Anxiety is being afraid to raise your hand in class because you may or may not have pit stains, and if you do then everyone will see and they'll tease. Then you'll be the topic of discussion at your class reunion ten or fifteen years down the line. Anxiety is being sick to your stomach as your mind races about all the wrong ways someone might have interpreted your text messages. Anxiety is not knowing whether or not to address someone as Mrs. or Ms., so you avoid talking to them at all. Anxiety is always thinking you did something wrong even though you know you did everything right. Anxiety is forcing yourself to sleep at night while your mind decides to start calculating bad grades, replaying old embarrassing conversations and making up scenarios that may never happen. This may all sound ridiculous but it is all very real. Now, imagine suffering from both depression and anxiety at the same time— your depression is keeping you down and your anxiety is causing you to worry about your depression keeping you down... sounds fun, right? This shit is literally the worst, and I wouldn't wish it on my worst enemy.

It wasn't until after my second suicidal thought that I knew it was time I sought out help—professional help. I needed to talk to someone who knew nothing about me, therefore, there was no judgment or predispositions. I needed to talk to someone who actually knew how to respond to my illness, and not someone who could only assume. Unfortunately, I didn't receive proper help until my senior year in college where I met Miss Emily, my counselor. I felt as though my parents didn't read too deep into anything that concerned me. Whatever they saw on the surface is how they interpreted the entire situation, so they didn't recognize how desperately I needed counseling. Honestly, I feared them. Not because they'd hurt me physically, but because of what they'd think of me.

I have a really close girlfriend who had felt the same way about her parents. We built a relationship based off of conversation that distinctly dealt with our relationship with our mom and dad. Her fear of disappointing her parents had lied just as deep as mine. So much so, that she hid a pregnancy and an abortion from them. She had slipped up and gotten herself into one of the scariest situations she'd ever been in. She was around four weeks pregnant when she'd randomly taken three pregnancy tests to explain why she'd been seven days late on her period. She called me crying her eyes out, in such emotional pain that I could feel it through the phone. Her guy wasn't the most comforting, nor was he the most understanding and that did nothing but cause her to panic more. She and I spent the entire day on the phone as she cried herself to a state of exhaustion. She knew she didn't want a child right now and she definitely wasn't prepared to take care of one financially. All of the love in the world can't support a baby as it should be supported. So abortion was the one and only option. It was also mutually agreed upon between her and her dude. I told her to look into medical abortions, taking the pill should be much less invasive and you can do it in the comfort of your own home. Once we did the research, she decided it was what she was most comfortable with. It was also the easiest to hide from her parents. I asked her if she was really sure this was something she wanted to keep from them, or at least from her mother. But she explained to me how she couldn't take facing the disappointment; she had never messed up this bad. No matter how many times she'd say how badly she wanted her mother, she could never bring herself to telling her.

I was heartbroken. She couldn't handle this situation and there was nothing I could do for her except be there. I pitched in, along with a few of her closest cousins, and helped out with the abortion money. That gave her a bit of relief, and that gave me a bit of relief. She hadn't even had the abortion yet, but it was already taking a toll on her. She had sunk deeper into her depression; she was hollow and cold. I talked her off the ledge three times one day! To think that she'd prefer death over her situation hurt me like hell. We had only one week of school left so, it would be over soon. But, I won't get into the gory details of the abortion in itself out of respect for her. However, today she is okay, physically, but is still affected emotionally.

Just like my homegirl, I didn't want to make my parents and I look flawed as a family and I didn't feel like explaining what was going on with me to the two people who were supposed to know me best. However, since attending my counseling sessions with my girl, Miss Emily, I have been at my healthiest, mentally and emotionally. So to Miss Emily, thank you. You may not be aware of the role you've played in my life these past few months, but you have been vital in my psychological restoration. I thank God for you a million and one times.

To my readers that can relate to this chapter the most or know of someone who has experienced some of the same things, open your mouths and speak. With cases like this silence is literally deadly. Don't be too prideful to ask for help, there is nothing embarrassing about taking care of yourself. Remember, you have a responsibility to yourself to do so— To my young, brown men, especially. Masculinity in today's society equivocates to control, lack of sensitivity, tough shells and tough cores, sustainability, mental and physical strength. So, imagine how a man may feel knowing that the one thing he is supposed to have control over, he can't seem to grip for shit. Asking for help is rarely the first option a man chooses, but when it comes to mental and emotional instability, it's critical. CRITICAL, ESPECIALLY FOR THE BLACK MAN. As magical as you are, the world only sees you as a cheap act. Every chance they get to tear you down, they'll take it. So, at least shield your mind and your spirit when it's in its most vulnerable state. Seek help. Talk to someone. Be the best version of the man you want to be.

As a brown girl who suffers from anxiety and depression, I'm insecure about everything from my body to my talents. Every guy I've dated or dealt with has broken my heart so I do not trust easily, but somehow still find myself loving the same. I don't have the best relationship with my parents and for a while, I didn't have the strongest relationship with God, yet I somehow remained prayerful. While also being a black woman who comes from a Christian background, the words "depressed" and "prayerful" aren't expected to be in the same sentence. Well, let me make something clear for all the saved and sanctified folk out there: PRAYER HEALS THE SPIRIT. COUNSELING HEALS THE MIND. MEDICINE HEALS THE BODY. You can believe and pray all you want, but faith without works is dead. Pray and do. Pray and seek help from other resources.

Damn. This was probably the hardest chapter for me to write. Before now, Only three people knew about my struggle with mental health. Now, everydamnbody knows. But, that's what this piece of work is all about. There are more and more young, brown girls who are speaking the fuck up about the reality of things. I'm just here to lend my voice, my happiness, my truth, my pain, my proverb. This was some sad shit, but fortunately enough for me, I'm living throughout my happy ending. Therefore, if God did it for me, He'll do it for you.

6. RELEASE

This is reflection time.

Here's where I want you to glance over what you just read and see how your perspective has changed.

Let's start here:

I, _____, **honor my proverb. It has (name three ways in which your journey has helped you)**

_____,

_____, **and**

_____.

Before reading this book *I* (state where were you on the course of your journey in regards to mindset, spirituality, etc.?)

_____

_____

_____

_____.

After reading this book *I*

_____

_____

_____

_____.

Moving forward *I* (state your plans for your future—
How will you grow? How will your environment
change? Who will you bring along or leave behind?,
etc.)

_____

_____

_____

_____

_____

_____.

My proverb is (give three adjectives to describe your
story/proverb) _____,

_____, and

_____. Every situation I have
encountered in the past has shaped me into the
person that I am now so that I'd be able to fit
perfectly into the situations of today. I applaud
myself for never giving up. I applaud myself for
never giving in. This is a promise to myself, that for
as long as I live, I'll never silence myself or discredit
my growth.

sign here

X

Look at you. Growing and shit.
I believe reflection and reconstruction are two of the most vital parts of growth. How will you ever become better if you never pay attention to the things that are holding you back? Sure, reflection isn't always easy. It will be some shit that you honestly don't *want* to remember. It will also be some shit that you don't want to *admit*. But, the outcome of recognizing those things and making the appropriate adjustments is always going to be beneficial.

7. PROVERB 31:25

She is clothed with strength and dignity and she laughs without fear of the future.

Ha! Look at ya girl, livin' and shit. Never in a million and twenty-one years did I think I'd actually be writing a book. I've wanted to for years, but I never convinced myself to sit my ass down and *do* it. I am thankful for challenge, for growth, for change and for new things. I was thinking I'd dedicate this *entire* chapter to myself and all that my strength and dignity have allowed me to overcome. However, I thought I'd dedicate majority of this last chapter to the women in my life who have helped me heal. Whether it had just been a conversation, or a physical reaching out, I thank you for your genuine concern for my well being and in return I'd like to commend you on your growth. So here's to you. Here's to your proverb.

To my greatest gift of family and friendship, Tootie.

From church babies to best friends twenty years later. Our mothers sistership made us cousins, but God made us for one another. I never met someone as similar to me as you. I never met another female as genuine as you. I never felt a friendship as comfortable and safe as ours. In this short amount of time of reconnection, I've seen you grow *with* me and *for* yourself. We've battled a lot of the same demons and it has allowed us to heal in the same ways— through our talents. You've inspired me to put forth all my energy into the one thing that will never fail me unless I allow it to. My businesses and newfound goals and dreams have been ignited by a lot of what you've said to me. I'd never witnessed someone pray for me, though I've always heard the promise from few fellows. I thank God for gifting you to me and me to you all the time. Not only do I get to reap the benefits of your love and friendship, but I get to reciprocate and watch you flourish as well—and trust me, it's just as exciting. You and I are the same person. Same minds and same spirits. Therefore, I know exactly what light to speak into you because it is the same light I've yearned for to be spoken into myself. I wish you nothing but continuous growth spiritually, mentally and emotionally. I commend you on the decisions that you've made as a young business woman and, most importantly, as a young *black* woman. I've been blessed many times throughout my life, but you my dear, have been one of the most valued. I love you Tootie. Forever and ever.

To the one I pray I never have to live without, Georgie Striblet.

"Baby, these people ain't worth a blow from yo nose!"

      I believe that grandparents are the greatest gifts on earth. Fortunately, I've been blessed to have time spent getting to know and love all four of my grandparents. However, my closet angel on earth is my gramma, Mrs. Georgie Mae Striblet. Mama, I love you! You are the safest person I can talk to. You are the only person who can brighten my day no matter *what*. You've sat on the phone with me while I've cried to you about everything from being hungry to relationship breakups and everything else. Your love is unmatched. I pray I leave before you do because life without you is unimaginable. I've talked myself out of very trying situations all for the sake of how you'd feel. I commend you for remaining as selfless as you have even whilst being used and sometimes abused by the ones that are closest to you. I want to give love like you one day. It is truly magical. Please don't leave me before I make it big. I love you gramma and I promise to never call you "granny".

To my sunflower, Andrea.

Since I got the chance to call you my friend, God revealed that you were much more. You are my guardian angel. Somehow you could sense when I needed you most and you made yourself as available as you could. You were the truest definition of a friend. You've sat with me through the toughest breakup of my life. You've talked me off of ledges and probably had no clue. You've been extremely encouraging and supportive of my businesses and my dreams. You have the ability to make me feel like I'm on top of the world even when I feel like I'm at the bottom of the pit. You are *love* in its purest form. I am just as proud of you as you are of me. You are undoubtedly one of the strongest young women I know for countless reasons. I look up to you. You inspire me to be better. I commend you for creating your own organization on campus. I commend you for starting your own business(*es*). I commend you for overcoming your demons. I commend you for remaining such an untarnished person even while enduring some very tarnishing situations.

To my mentors, Candice and Genesha.

First off, "heeyyyyyyyy mentorrrrrrrr." Again, God did his thing with these blessings, right here. I have literally sent manuscripts to each of you about my fears of the future, my new adventures, my trials and tribulations, my accomplishments, everything. Thankfully enough, you didn't see me as this crazy, annoying young woman, but instead you embraced me and all that I came with, with open arms. I ran everything by the both of you waiting for a "that sounds great" or a "maybe you should try this instead". I had never had mentors before you two and I don't know how I'd been making it without one before you two came along. You two are so admirable. I commend you on your many successes. I commend you on never feeling as though it's too late for you to follow your dreams and reach new heights. I love you both. I hope I'm making you proud.

To my twin, Mia.

There was a moment in time where I thought the two of us would never end up friends, let alone as close as we are now. Not because there were ever any ill vibes, but because we never ran in the same circles. But to my suprise, you are one of my closest friends and you and I *both* know I don't have too many of those. We've had our ups and downs but you've quickly earned *I'm not one to play with* and that I take friendship very seriously. Honestly, I'd kill for you. You have seen my cry, you've seen me at my lowest and have enjoyed my highs right alongside me. You were the only person that would come to my dorm room just to sit in silence. That's really all we needed from one another: company and silence. You were one of the only people to sew into my clothing line, rocking your choker like it was the hottest thing on the block, baby! I love how you've blossomed since our friendship. I'm glad I could play a part in you learning to love yourself more. I commend you for opening yourself up to new things. I commend you for recognizing your voice and its power. I love you, bitch!

To my sis, Bri-Skee.

> *"You will always have a friend in me. Just a text away. Don't hesitate...- Bri"*

I always heard people say how *real* friends can withstand long seasons of physical and vocal distance, but I never agreed with it... until I met you. From our Junior year at PSM to our Senior years in college you have remained the same. You've somehow managed to lend me just the right amount of love and encouragement as often as you possibly can at all the right moments. You were also one of those friendships I never saw coming but am beyond grateful to have. You are one of the people I'm inspired by the most in my life. You've achieved so much since I've last seen you. Traveling and expanding your education. I commend you for following your heart and staying on track of every plan you've made for your life thus far. You are a gem. You are my friend. You are my sister.

To Miracle and Jayla, three the hard way.

Thank you. You saved me. It'll always be us three against the world. God gave me the best gifts in cousins and then decided to also give me the best gifts in friendship. I am so proud of the both of you. You are two of the most confident young women I've ever known and I've always admired that. Super strong, super talented, super beautiful. I love you two beyond measures. Keep being great throughout all of your endeavors. It feels good to know that even when it feels like no one is in the crowd, there'll always be at least *two* seated upfront. Forever and always, THREE THE HARD WAY.

To my babies, my younger sisters.

We don't share the same blood, but I've been in each of you alls lives since the moment you were born. If anyone asks me, YES, I am a big sister to six of the most amazing young girls. In moments where I feel as if I'm doing all of this for *nothing,* I remember I have six very important reasons and I get up and do what I need to do. Y'all are my best friends and honestly my own kids are gonna have the toughest competition! Y'all are the prettiest, smartest, sweetest, funniest, people I know— from my oldest baby, Mo, to my youngest baby, Jamesha. I hope that more than anything, I make y'all proud to call me your big sister.

To my mama.

A apologize for every moment where I thought I knew the most, for every time I made you feel like you knew nothing and for every call I didn't pick up. I will admit, you have your downfalls as a "person" but you made up for those as a "Mommy". We've never been the *best* of friends, but you've always been the one to count on. We've never shared the deepest of secrets but I will forever appreciate your willingness to know, even when I didn't want you to— I knew you at least cared. I'm sure for the next 21 years I'll be just as stubborn and independent as I am now, but I'll definitely be less apprehensive to letting you voice your opinion… because I don't know it all. I commend you on being the first example of a business woman I ever had. I owe a lot of my drive and work ethic to you. I commend you for handling marriage as best you can, despite marriage not handling you the best it could. I commend you for everything. Literally, you do it all. I love you mama.

To my biggest competition, Myself.

You've put me through some shit but you've also helped see me through everything. I used to think you were useless, but ironically you were the most useful tool along my entire journey. After all these years of thinking you weren't enough, you were actually everything that I needed. You are amazing, sweetie. I love you more than anything. I commend you for sticking things out even when they were hurting you the most. I commend you for restoring your relationship with God. I commend you for picking yourself up after being pushed so far down. I especially commend you for writing this book and diving into each and every one of your talents. You are truly, *that* bitch. For every moment I didn't love you correctly, I'll be sure to make it up to you. Be great, you don't have any other option.

These were not the only women who have helped me throughout my journey, so to everyone of you, thank you. You know who are... and who you are *not*. I have not forgotten the men in my life that have helped me as well. I love you all immensely. I hope that you all have learned from and were able to relate to all that you've read. I sat out to do one job and that was to lend comfort. Comfort in knowing that there is someone who understands. Comfort in knowing that you were never alone. Comfort in knowing that you'll always have someone who'll listen. I thank you for sticking around until the end.

Favor, Peace and Blessings,
Mimi.

Made in the USA
Lexington, KY
30 July 2018